ALL ABOUT ARACHNIDS
HUNTSMAN SPIDERS

by Jenna Lee Gleisner

pogo

Ideas for Parents and Teachers

Pogo Books let children practice reading informational text while introducing them to nonfiction features such as headings, labels, sidebars, maps, and diagrams, as well as a table of contents, glossary, and index.

Carefully leveled text with a strong photo match offers early fluent readers the support they need to succeed.

Before Reading

- "Walk" through the book and point out the various nonfiction features. Ask the student what purpose each feature serves.
- Look at the glossary together. Read and discuss the words.

Read the Book

- Have the child read the book independently.
- Invite them to list questions that arise from reading.

After Reading

- Discuss the child's questions. Talk about how they might find answers to those questions.
- Prompt the child to think more. Ask: Huntsman spiders hunt their prey instead of catching them in webs. Can you name any other spiders that hunt their prey?

Pogo Books are published by Jump!
5357 Penn Avenue South
Minneapolis, MN 55419
www.jumplibrary.com

Copyright © 2025 Jump!
International copyright reserved in all countries. No part of this book may be reproduced in any form without written permission from the publisher.

Library of Congress Cataloging-in-Publication Data

Names: Gleisner, Jenna Lee, author.
Title: Huntsman spiders / by Jenna Lee Gleisner.
Description: Minneapolis, MN: Jump!, Inc., [2025]
Series: All about arachnids | Includes index.
Audience: Ages 7-10
Identifiers: LCCN 2024032925 (print)
LCCN 2024032926 (ebook)
ISBN 9798892136150 (hardcover)
ISBN 9798892136167 (paperback)
ISBN 9798892136174 (ebook)
Subjects: LCSH: Huntsman spiders–Juvenile literature.
Classification: LCC QL458.42.S63 G54 2025 (print)
LCC QL458.42.S63 (ebook)
DDC 595.4/4–dc23/eng/20240830
LC record available at https://lccn.loc.gov/2024032925
LC ebook record available at https://lccn.loc.gov/2024032926

Editor: Katie Chanez
Designer: Emma Almgren-Bersie

Photo Credits: Danut Vieru/Shutterstock, cover; holgs/iStock, 1; Bebenjy/iStock, 3; Moppet/iStock, 4; Pong Wira/Shutterstock, 5; Niney Azman/Shutterstock, 6-7; Chris Howes/Wild Places Photography/Alamy, 8-9; Ken Griffiths/iStock, 10; Photoshot - NHPA/SuperStock, 11; Gillian08/Dreamstime, 12-13; imageBROKER GmbH & Co. KG/Alamy, 14; kurt_G/Shutterstock, 15; Ivan Andersen/Alamy, 16-17; Premaphotos/Alamy, 18-19; Kobus Peche/Alamy, 20-21; Florian DENIS/iStock, 23.

Printed in the United States of America at Corporate Graphics in North Mankato, Minnesota.

TABLE OF CONTENTS

CHAPTER 1
Long Legs...4

CHAPTER 2
Hiding at Home......................................10

CHAPTER 3
Mating and Molting..............................14

ACTIVITIES & TOOLS
Try This!...22
Glossary...23
Index..24
To Learn More.......................................24

CHAPTER 1
LONG LEGS

This spider is big. It is hairy. It looks like a tarantula but is not. What is this long-legged **arachnid**? It is a huntsman spider!

band

Many huntsman spiders have brown or black hair. They may have bands, or stripes, on their eight legs. These colors and patterns are **camouflage**.

CHAPTER 1 5

There are more than 1,300 huntsman spider **species**. All have long legs. These spiders do not spin webs to catch **prey**. Instead, they hunt. This is how they got their name. They use their long legs to chase prey.

CHAPTER 1

TAKE A LOOK!

What are the parts of a huntsman spider? Take a look!

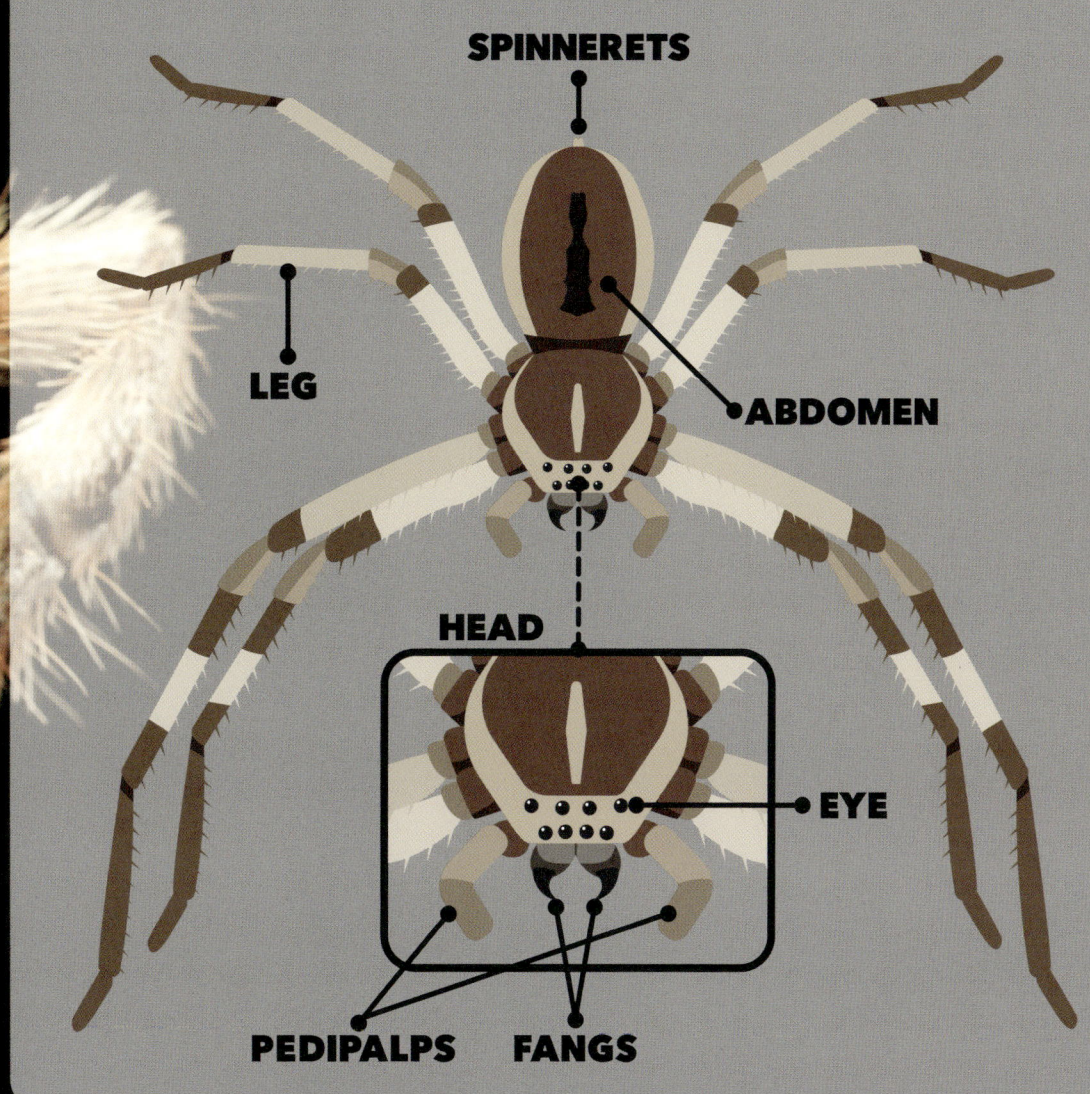

Many species have a **leg span** of up to five inches (13 centimeters). The giant huntsman is even larger! Its legs span 12 inches (30 cm) across. That is the size of a dinner plate! Its large, long legs make it a fast hunter. It can run three feet (0.9 meters) in just one second!

DID YOU KNOW?

Huntsman spiders hunt cockroaches and scorpions. Giant huntsman spiders catch even bigger prey. Like what? They eat mice, bats, and even lizards!

CHAPTER 1

CHAPTER 2
HIDING AT HOME

These spiders' legs go out to the sides. They have twisted **joints**. They can move side-to-side. They are sometimes called crab spiders.

Their legs help them flatten their bodies. Why? They like to hide. They fit on leaves and under rocks and tree bark.

CHAPTER 2

Huntsman spiders live in warm areas around the world. Many live in Australia. They are often found in cars and homes!

CHAPTER 2

TAKE A LOOK!

Where do huntsman spiders live? Take a look!

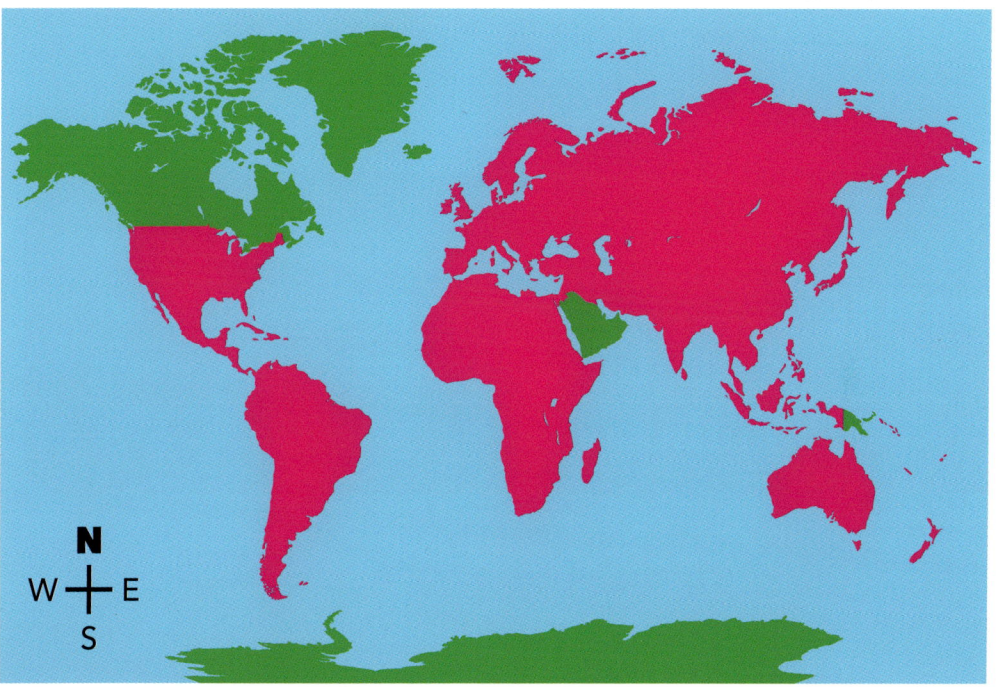

■ = huntsman spider range

CHAPTER 2 13

CHAPTER 3
MATING AND MOLTING

Some female spiders kill the male after **mating**. Not huntsman spiders! These spiders spend time together. They even pet one another.

Each species is different. After mating, some females carry their eggs in a sac.

egg sac

CHAPTER 3 15

Other females hide their egg sac under a rock or bark. They protect it with their lives. They do not leave the eggs. This means they may not eat for up to three weeks! What if a **predator** comes close? The female lifts her front legs. She looks even larger. She scares it away.

> ### DID YOU KNOW?
>
> What eats huntsman spiders? Predators include birds and geckoes. Spider wasps will also eat these spiders.

CHAPTER 3

It is time to hatch! **Spiderlings** come out of the egg sac. They are very light in color. They stay with mom for many weeks.

DID YOU KNOW?

Most huntsman spiders live alone. But a few species live in **colonies**. A colony can have hundreds of spiders. They share prey. They help raise each other's young.

CHAPTER 3

Spiderlings **molt** many times. Each time, they grow bigger and darker. They grow up and hunt on their own!

DID YOU KNOW?

Huntsman spiders do not live long. Their **lifespan** is about two years.

ACTIVITIES & TOOLS

TRY THIS!

MEASURE YOUR ARM SPAN

The giant huntsman spider has the largest leg span of any spider. It is 12 inches (30 cm) across! Measure your arm span to see how you compare to a huntsman in this fun activity!

What You Need:
- a few friends
- measuring tape
- pencil and paper

1. Have one friend stand with their arms stretched out fully to the sides. Using the measuring tape, measure the distance between the tip of each middle finger. Write down how many inches the friend's arm span is.

2. Repeat this for your other friends. Then have one of the friends measure your arm span and write it down.

3. Who has the shortest arm span? Who has the longest? How do the arm spans compare to a giant huntsman spider's leg span?

GLOSSARY

arachnid: A creature with a body divided into two parts, such as a spider or a scorpion.

camouflage: A disguise or natural coloring that allows animals to hide by making them look like their surroundings.

colonies: Groups of spiders that live together.

joints: Places in the body where two or more pieces meet to allow movement.

leg span: The distance between the tips of a spider's legs.

lifespan: How long something usually lives.

mating: Coming together to produce babies.

molt: To shed an outer layer.

predator: An animal that hunts other animals for food.

prey: Animals hunted by other animals for food.

species: One of the groups into which similar animals and plants are divided.

spiderlings: Baby spiders.

ACTIVITIES & TOOLS

INDEX

Australia 12
camouflage 5
chase 6
colonies 19
egg sac 15, 16, 19
hairy 4, 5
hatch 19
hide 11, 16
hunt 6, 9, 20
joints 10

legs 5, 6, 7, 9, 10, 11, 16
lifespan 20
mating 14, 15
molt 20
predator 16
prey 6, 9, 19
range 13
run 9
species 6, 9, 15, 19
spiderlings 19, 20

TO LEARN MORE

Finding more information is as easy as 1, 2, 3.
1. Go to www.factsurfer.com
2. Enter "huntsmanspiders" into the search box.
3. Choose your book to see a list of websites.